JOHANNACASLER
Fitness

MMM!
METABOLIC
MAKEOVER
MEALS
C O O K B O O K

by **Johanna Casler**
Fitness Trainer & Nutrition Specialist

WORKOUTS POWERED BY SCIENCE®

Introduction

A large portion of my Fitness & Wellness business is providing my clients customized nutritional support, tips and recipes. Since the market is flooded with a sea of inaccuracies and misguided literature regarding nutrition and calorie intake, I have assembled some of my most popular recipes to empower you with science-infused knowledge to help you make better dietary decisions.

Our metabolism declines as we age, so you need to take action in both exercise and nutrition to slow the decline. Calories we burn in exercise are important as they provide invaluable health benefits, and the calories we burn just existing are critical to long term health and weight management. Being a metabolic specialist, my recipes and tips are specifically created to improve your overall health and metabolism for the long run.

Over the years, I have been asked to combine my nutritional information and recipes into a book format, so I'm thrilled to introduce my first volume! I hope you find the information useful, easy to integrate into your daily diet and enjoy the new healthier you!

To your health!
Johanna Casler

Dedication

I dedicate this book to my loyal clients who have supported my business efforts and encouraged me to put these nutrition tips and recipes into this book.

Table of Contents

ENTREES

Easy Cheesy Chicken	2
Bok Choy Booster	4
Hearts & Soul	6
The Reel Deal	8
Sweet & Spicy Salmon	10
Asian Medley	12
Protein Skewers	14
Skinny Mini Tacos	16

SALADS

Sumptuous Salad	18
Naked Salad	20
Greek Beet Salad	22

ONE POT WONDERS

Carnitas Stew	24
Pot-O-Pasta	26
Souped Up V8	28
Kickin' Chicken Soup	30

SIDE DISHES

Herb Appeal	32
The Wild Side	34
Guiltless Pleasure	36
Heavenly Eggs	38

SNACKS

Mega Melons	40
Mighty Mouth Poppers	42
Energy Clusters	44
Fat Attack Snack	46
Power Cube Smoothie	48

INFUSED WATER

Strawberry Basil	50
Lemon Thyme Turmeric	50
Lemon Ginger Mint	50

ENTREES

GF

Gluten Free

Easy Cheesy Chicken

YIELDS: 4 servings | **SERVING SIZE:** 1 chicken breast

INGREDIENTS:

4	Thin Cut Chicken Breasts
4	Basil Leaves
12	Mozzarella Cheese Balls
1 tsp	Paprika
1 tsp	Almond Flour
1 cup	Marinara Sauce

PREPARATION:

Tear Basil leaf into 4 pieces and place with 3 mozzarella balls *(1 oz per breast)* on each chicken breast *(alternate like photo)*, then sprinkle with paprika. Roll the chicken breast to enclose the cheese and basil. Dust both sides of chicken breast with almond flour. Lightly spray baking pan with canola oil. Bake at 375° for 30 minutes. Serve with warm marinara sauce. *< photo shows before & after >*

RECIPE RATING:

1   2   3   4   5

NUTRITION POINTS:

Aprox 210 calories + 30 gm protein per serving

Almond flour is gluten free and has heart health benefits **Mozzarella** has healthy fat and calcium that helps you lose fat **Basil** is a super herb with a host of health benefits, just ½ cup provides 98% of the daily value of vitamin K **Paprika** is a power spice with anti-inflammatory benefits **Marinara** is packed with lycopene which has been linked to cancer & heart disease prevention. Lycopene is absorbed better from cooked tomatoes.

2

JOHANNACASLER *Fitness*

Easy Cheesy Chicken

ENTREES

Gluten Free

Bok Choy Booster

YIELDS: 4 servings | **SERVING SIZE:** 2 cups

INGREDIENTS:
1 lb	Stir Fry Meat, cut up
1 cup	Broccolini, chopped
1 cup	Carrots, chopped
1 cup	Baby Bok Choy, chopped
¼ cup	Basil leaves
1 ea	Jalapeño, chopped 🔥
1 ea	Serrano Pepper, chopped 🔥
1 cup	Tamari *(gluten free soy sauce)*

PREPARATION:
Place meat in medium hot skillet. Add bok choy, carrots & broccolini to the skillet. Top with basil, sliced jalapeño and red serrano pepper. Pour tamari sauce over the contents of pan. Cook uncovered on medium heat for approximately 20 minutes, until meat is done.

RECIPE RATING:

1   2   3   4   5

NUTRITION POINTS:
Aprox 214 calories + 27 gm protein per serving

Bok choy is one of the highest ranked vegetables with 21 nutrients **Broccolini** is a cross between broccoli and Chinese broccoli and is a great source of vitamins A & C **Carrot** nutrients are best absorbed when cooked and provide a good source of Lycopene **Hot Peppers** have a compound called capsaicin which fights inflammation and it can also give your metabolism a boost!

JOHANNACASLER
Fitness

Bok Choy Booster

www.JohannaCasler.com

ENTREES

Hearts & Soul

YIELDS: 4 servings | **SERVING SIZE:** 2 cups

INGREDIENTS:
3 cups High Protein Penne Pasta
1 can   Artichoke Hearts
2 cups Frozen Chopped Spinach
1 large Red Jalapeño Pepper, chopped 🔥
½ cup   Parmesan Cheese
4 cups Water

PREPARATION:
Place all ingredients in baking pan. Pour water over the ingredients. Bake at 375° for 10 minutes. Stir, then bake another 10 minutes, until pasta is done. *< photo shows before & after >*

RECIPE RATING:

1   2   3   4   5

NUTRITION POINTS:
Aprox 200 calories + 22 gm protein per serving

Artichokes are antioxidant super heroes, they are listed as number 7 on the USDA's top 20 antioxidant-rich foods. They are a great source of folic acid, vitamins B, C & D as well as the minerals potassium, copper and iron. They are naturally low in calories with 1 cup equaling only 30 calories • **Spinach** is a super green and the powerful nutrients are absorbed better when cooked.

6

JOHANNACASLER
Fitness

Hearts
&
Soul

ENTREES

Gluten Free

The Reel Deal

YIELDS: 2 servings | **SERVING SIZE:** 5 oz

INGREDIENTS:

10 oz	Swordfish
1 ea	Juice of whole Lemon
1 ea	Juice of whole Lime
1 tbs	Avocado Oil
1 tsp	Oregano, minced
1 tsp	Italian Parsley, minced
1 tsp	Turmeric, ground
1 tsp	Thyme

PREPARATION:

Combine lemon and lime juices with all spices in a bowl, mix well. Brush mix over whole fish. Grill fish over medium heat for approximately 5 minutes per side for medium cooked.

RECIPE RATING:

1 2 3 4 5

NUTRITION POINTS:

Aprox 250 calories + 27 gm protein per serving per serving

Fish has a long list of health benefits. Research has linked eating fish to improved brain health • **Lemons** help cleanse the liver and have antioxidants • **Limes** are being looked at more closely for their anti-cancer fighting compounds • **Avocado** oil is a healthy fat and great for high-heat cooking • **Oregano**, thyme and parsley are super herbs since they are a rich source of vitamin K and contain a very high concentration of antioxidants. They also have strong antibacterial properties and anti-inflammatory properties as well.

JOHANNACASLER
Fitness

The
Reel Deal

Gluten Free

Sweet & Spicy Salmon

YIELDS: 2 servings | **SERVING SIZE:** 5 oz

INGREDIENTS:
10 oz   Salmon per serving
2 tsp   Apricot Jam
½ tsp   Cayenne Pepper, ground
1 tsp   Turmeric, ground

PREPARATION:
Sprinkle both sides of salmon with cayenne and tumeric, spread jam on top of fish, place on cedar plank *(soak plank in water for 1hr before grilling)* or place on heavy foil, lightly sprayed with canola oil. Grill over medium heat for 10-12 minutes for medium cooked.

RECIPE RATING:

☆ ☆ ☆ ☆ ☆
1 2 3 4 5

NUTRITION POINTS:
Aprox 175 calories + 24 gm protein per serving

Salmon is an excellent source of omega-3 fatty acids including both EPA and DHA fatty acids. EPH fatty acids work to prevent unwanted inflammation. DHA fatty acid is essential for maintenance of brain health • **Cayenne Pepper** has many benefits including increased circulation which boosts metabolism. It contains high levels of beta-carotene which boost immunity. It also contains antibacterial properties as well as helps stabilize blood sugar • **Turmeric** has a host of health benefits from aiding in brain health to alleviating joint pain with its powerful anti-inflammatory properties.

JOHANNACASLER
Fitness

SWEET
& SPICY
SALMON

ENTREES

Gluten Free

Asian Medley

YIELDS: 4 servings | **SERVING SIZE:** 1 cup + 3 oz protein

INGREDIENTS:

2 cups Basmati Brown Rice
1 cup Broccoli, chopped
1 cup Zucchini, chopped
1 cup Tamari *(gluten free soy sauce)*
1 tbsp Fresh Ginger, grated
2 tbsp Toasted Sesame Seeds
1 cup Vegetable Broth
1 tbsp Sesame Oil
3 oz Chicken, Salmon or Steak per serving
1 tbsp Tamari

RECIPE RATING:

⭐ ⭐ ⭐ ⭐ ⭐
1   2   3   4   5

PREPARATION:

Place rice and vegetables in a skillet. Pour cup of tamari, cup of broth and sesame oil over rice and vegetables. Bring mixture to a boil, then reduce heat to medium and cook for approximately 10 minutes. Sprinkle vegetables with 1 tbsp of toasted sesame seeds. Grill and serve with your favorite protein source marinated with 1 tbsp tamari and 1 tbsp sesame seeds. *< photo shows with & without chicken >*

NUTRITION POINTS:

Aprox 430 calories + 30 gm protein per serving

Ginger promotes digestion and has powerful anti-inflammatory properties. Studies show regular consumption of ginger can give relief of muscle and joint pain · **Sesame seeds** are a good source of minerals such as calcium and iron. The fiber found in sesame seeds has been found to reduce cholesterol and promote liver health. An ounce is loaded with vitamin D and as much calcium as a glass of milk, both help a body's fat burning capabilities.

JOHANNACASLER
Fitness

ASIAN MEDLEY

Gluten Free

Protein Skewers

YIELDS: 3 servings | **SERVING SIZE:** 2 skewers

INGREDIENTS:
1 lb   Boneless Chicken Breasts
½ cup   Watercress, minced
½ cup   Chives, minced
1 tbsp   Garlic, crushed
2 tbsp   Avocado Oil

PREPARATION:
Cut chicken into 1" cubes. Mix watercress, chives, garlic and avocado oil in a bowl. Put chicken in bowl, mix well to coat. Marinate in refrigerator for at least 20 minutes, then skewer chicken pieces and place on non-stick pan. Bake at 400° for 25 minutes. You can also grill for 8 minutes, turn and grill an additional 6 minutes.

RECIPE RATING:

1   2   3   4   5

NUTRITION POINTS:
Aprox 240 calories + 40 gm protein per serving

Watercress is truly a super food. Research shows this power green ranks highest in providing nutrients that reduce chronic disease. It earned a perfect score of 100 ANDI score *(Aggregate Nutrient Density Score)*. Eat it raw or cooked with only 4 calories per cup • **Chives** are high in vitamins A, C & K. They are a good source of iron, calcium and fiber as well as anti-inflammatory, antibiotic, antibacterial, antiviral and antimicrobial properties.

JOHANNACASLER
Fitness

Protein Skewers

Skinny Mini Tacos

YIELDS: 3 servings | **SERVING SIZE:** 3 tacos

INGREDIENTS:
1 lb   Lean Ground Hamburger
1 cup   Your favorite Salsa
1 pkg   Wonton Wrappers
1 ea   Jalapeño, sliced

PREPARATION:
Brown hamburger and drain excess fat. Mix hamburger with salsa in a bowl. Spray both sides of wonton wrappers with canola cooking spray. Place two overlapped wrappers in each muffin tin. Spoon taco mix into wrappers, top with cheese and jalapeños. Bake at 375° for 10 minutes, or until wrappers are golden brown.

RECIPE RATING:
☆ ☆ ☆ ☆ ☆
1   2   3   4   5

NUTRITION POINTS:
Aprox 210 calories + 24 gm protein per serving

Wonton Wrappers are only 17 calories per wrapper making for a great low calorie alternative to traditional taco shells • **Salsa** adds flavor, vitamins such as lycopene and is very low in calories • **Jalapeños** gives spice with a metabolism boost and are naturally low in calories.

Skinny Mini
TACOS

SALADS

Gluten Free

Sumptuous Salad

YIELDS: 1 serving

INGREDIENTS:

4 oz   Fresh Cod
1 tbsp   Miso Paste
2 cups   Mixed Power Greens *(Spinach, Kale, Chard)*
1 cup   Pear, chopped
1 tbsp   Walnuts, chopped
1 tsp   Cinnamon, ground
¼ tsp   Cayenne Pepper, ground 🔥

PREPARATION:

Lightly spray pan with canola oil, then brush miso paste on cod. Bake at 375° for aprox 15 minutes. In a bowl, toss pear, walnuts, cayenne and cinnamon, then add to pan and bake another 5 minutes. Place all ingredients in bowl and toss. *No dressing needed as the pear, spices and miso provide plenty of flavor.*

RECIPE RATING:

1   2   3   4   5

NUTRITION POINTS:

Aprox 350 calories + 30 gm protein per serving

Pears have more fiber than any other fruit. This fall fruit adds a sweet kick • **Cinnamon** helps stabilize blood sugar • **Cayenne Pepper** has been associated with a wide range of health benefits including stimulating the circulatory system which can boost metabolism and help remove toxins from the body • **Walnuts** are a great source of vitamin E, omega-3 fats and antioxidants • **Fermented foods**, such as miso, contribute good bacteria for gut health • **Cod** is a mild and versatile white fish available throughout the year.

JOHANNACASLER
Fitness

Sumptuous
SALAD

SALADS

Gluten Free

Naked Salad

YIELDS: 1 serving

INGREDIENTS:
1 cup Chicken, cooked & chopped
½ cup Arugula
½ cup Apple, chopped
½ tsp Black Pepper
½ tsp Ground Cumin
½ Avocado

PREPARATION:
Chop cooked chicken into bite size pieces. Combine chicken, apples, cumin, black pepper and arugula in bowl, toss to mix. Place mixture in ½ avocado. *No dressing needed.*

RECIPE RATING:

1 2 3 4 5

NUTRITION POINTS:
Aprox 200 calories + 20 gm protein per serving

Avocados are truly a super food to be consumed often. They are loaded with heart healthy fat and have more potassium than a banana. New studies show they are powerful in fighting cancer cell growth **Sweet apples** add water-soluble fiber *(pectin)* and antioxidants **Arugula**, also know as "rocket salad", provides many of the same health benefits as kale, brussels sprouts and spinach. It doesn't have to be cooked to enhance our body's nutrient absorption. 2 Cups of Arugula has only 10 calories **Chicken** gives this salad a lean protein boost.

Naked
SALAD

SALADS

Greek Beet Salad

YIELDS: 1 serving

INGREDIENTS:

2 cups Baby Romaine Lettuce
½ cup Roasted Beets, cubed *(available pre-made)*
½ cup Watermelon Radishes, sliced thin
¼ cup Feta Cheese
1 tbs Olive Oil
1 tsp Balsamic Vinegar

PREPARATION:

Combine roasted beets, watermelon radishes and feta cheese with baby romaine lettuce. Drizzle oil and vinegar over salad, toss to coat.

RECIPE RATING:

1   2   3   4   5

NUTRITION POINTS:

Aprox 300 calories + 10 gm protein per serving

Romaine Lettuce is a low calorie, nutrient dense food *(with 80 nutrients)*. It is a great source of vitamins A, B1, C, K & folate. It is also a good source of the minerals manganese, potassium, copper & iron • **Beets** have a host of vitamins and minerals and contain phytonutrients that provide antioxidant, anti-inflammatory & detoxification support • **Radishes** are a rich source of the important nutrients lutein and beta-carotene • **Feta Cheese** is made from sheep or goat's milk. It provides a protein boost and is a good source of vitamin B12 and calcium. The fat in the cheese and olive oil are a healthy fat that helps you absorb the fat soluble vitamins A & K.

JOHANNACASLER *Fitness*

GREEK BEET SALAD

Gluten Free

Carnitas Stew

YIELDS: 8 servings | **SERVING SIZE:** 2 cups

INGREDIENTS:
2 lb	Pork Tenderloins
8 oz	Roasted Corn
8 oz	Diced Green Chilies
24 oz	Your favorite Salsa
2 tbsp	Cumin, ground or whole
1 ea	Jalapeño, chopped *(optional for extra spice)* 🔥
1 ea	Serrano Pepper, chopped *(optional for extra spice)* 🔥

PREPARATION:
Place tenderloins in slow cooker. Pour salsa over meat, add corn, green chilies, cumin and peppers. Cook on high for 4 hours. *This is a hearty meal for busy weeknights and great for leftovers.*

RECIPE RATING:

1   2   3   4   5

NUTRITION POINTS:
Aprox 175 calories + 24 gm protein per serving

Pork Tenderloin is a lean meat and nice alternative to chicken • **Cumin** is the star seasoning of this dish. It's a great source of iron and aids in digestion. Studies have shown it has anti-carcinogenic properties which could protect against cancer and helps with liver detoxification • **Salsa** adds loads of flavor and nutrients for very little calories. Tomatoes offer a great source of lycopene and when cooked allow for improved nutrient absorption.

JOHANNACASLER
Fitness

Carnitas STEW

ONE POT WONDERS

Pot-O-Pasta

YIELDS: 4 servings | **SERVING SIZE:** 2 cups

INGREDIENTS:

3 cups	Penne Pasta
2 ea	Garlic Cloves
2 cups	Fresh Spinach
1½ cups	Multi-colored Julienne Carrots
1 cup	Cherry Tomatoes
1 tsp	Fresh Thyme
1 tsp	Italian Parsley
1 tsp	Oregano
6 cups	Bone Broth or Water

PREPARATION:

Combine penne pasta, garlic cloves, spinach, carrots, thyme, Italian parsley and oregano in a slow cooker. Use bone broth for a protein boost, or water for a vegetarian version. Cook on low for 3 hours.

RECIPE RATING:

1 2 3 4 5

NUTRITION POINTS:

Aprox 175 calories + 16 gm of protein per serving *(w/ bone broth)*
Aprox 125 calories + 6 gm protein per serving *(vegetarian)*

Important Nutrients from tomatoes, spinach and carrots are absorbed better when cooked • **Herbs** offer a host of health benefits such as being antibacterial, antioxidant and anti-fungal. They contribute almost no calories but add extra flavor to your meals. Fresh herbs are best, when available. Most herbs are easy to grow yourself in small containers • **Bone Broth** gives a big protein boost as compared to regular broth and has very few calories.

JOHANNACASLER
Fitness

POT
-O-
PASTA

Gluten Free

Souped Up V8

YIELDS: 8 servings | **SERVING SIZE:** 2 cups

INGREDIENTS:
48 oz   Spicy Vegetable Juice bottle
1 cup   Bone Broth *(or vegatable)*
1 cup   Kale
1 cup   Broccoli, chopped
1 cup   Asparagus, cut
1 cup   Peas
1 cup   Carrots, chopped
1 cup   Potatoes, chopped
1 tbsp   Black Pepper
1 tbsp   Oregano, ground

PREPARATION:
Combine spicy vegetable juice, bone broth *(for vegetarian use vegetable broth)* and all other ingredients in slow cooker. Cook on low for 3 hours. *Top servings with parmesan cheese.*

RECIPE RATING:

1   2   3   4   5

NUTRITION POINTS:
Aprox 200 calories + 25 gm protein per serving *(w/ bone broth)*
Aprox 160 calories + 15 gm of protein per serving *(w/ veg broth)*

Spinach, Kale and Carrot nutrients are best absorbed when cooked **Spinach and Kale** are power greens that offer antioxidant properties. Both provide vitamin K which is very important to bone health **Peas** have higher protein content than any other vegetable and research is showing they have cancer fighting agents.

JOHANNACASLER
Fitness

Souped Up V8

ONE POT WONDERS

Gluten Free

Kickin' Chicken Soup

YIELDS: 8 servings | **SERVING SIZE:** 2 cups

INGREDIENTS:
30 oz	Chicken Broth
30 oz	Tomato Sauce
¼ cup	Worcestershire Sauce
3 ea	Boneless Chicken Breasts
2 cups	30-minute Brown Rice
4 ea	Garlic Cloves, chopped
1 tsp	Black Pepper
1 tsp	Cayenne Pepper, ground 🔥
¼ cup	Parmesan Cheese, gratetd

PREPARATION:
Place chicken in slow cooker. Combine all ingredients except rice, then stir to mix. Cook on high for 3 hours, adding rice at the last 30 minutes of cook time. *Top servings with parmesan cheese.*

RECIPE RATING:

1   2   3   4   5

NUTRITION POINTS:

Aprox 230 calories + 30 gm protein per serving

This is a **low calorie/high protein** dish that is naturally gluten free • **Tomato Sauce** is packed with lycopene, which is absorbed better in cooked tomatoes • **Garlic** is highly nutritious and very low in calories. It provides anti-inflammatory properties, combats hypertension and high cholesterol, as well as boosts the immune system • **Cayenne Pepper** is another star spice that is also a powerful antioxidant and immune booster.

JOHANNACASLER *Fitness*

KICKIN' CHICKEN SOUP

SIDE DISHES

Gluten Free

Herb Appeal

YIELDS: 4 servings | **SERVING SIZE:** 1 cup

INGREDIENTS:

14 oz	Quinoa Orzo
1 tsp	Italian Parsley, chopped
1 tsp	Basil, chopped
1 tsp	Oregano, chopped
1 tsp	Rosemary, minced
1 tsp	Thyme
1 tbs	Garlic Cloves, chopped
1 tbs	Olive Oil

PREPARATION:

Mix olive oil, herbs and garlic thoroughly, set aside. Cook quinoa orzo according to package directions. Drain the pasta, add the herb/garlic/oil mixture and toss to coat. Serve immediately for best taste and texture.

RECIPE RATING:

1   2   3   4   5

NUTRITION POINTS:

Aprox 200 calories + 6 gm protein per serving

Quinoa has experienced growing popularity because it is a gluten free, high nutrient grain. Unlike most grains, it is considered a complete protein. It can serve an important role in a gluten free or vegetarian diet • **Herbs** add flavor and nutrients with virtually no calories. They offer antibacterial, anti-fungal, antioxidant properties in addition to vitamins and minerals • **Olive Oil** has gained a reputation as a heart healthy oil contributing to overall health. It is best to use at room temperature or in low heat cooking since high heat breaks down the health benefit of the fat content.

JOHANNACASLER
Fitness

HERB
Appeal

SIDE DISHES

Gluten Free

The Wild Side

YIELDS: 4 servings | **SERVING SIZE:** 1 cup

INGREDIENTS:
2 cups	Wild Rice
1 ea	Zucchini, sliced
1 ea	Yellow Squash, sliced
1 cup	Broccoli, chopped
1 cup	Asparagus, cut
¼ cup	Parmesan Cheese
1 tbsp	Thyme

PREPARATION:
Cook rice according to package directions. Lightly spray pan with canola oil, add vegetables and roast for 10 minutes at 375°. Top rice with vegetables and parmesan cheese.

RECIPE RATING:

1   2   3   4   5

NUTRITION POINTS:
Aprox 175 calories + 10 gm protein per serving

This is a **low calorie** side dish that is naturally gluten free and high in fiber, vitamins and minerals **Wild Rice** is a great alternative to pasta or potatoes and is a great source of fiber **Lightly cooking** the vegetables keeps nutrients intact **Asparagus** has been shown to be metabolically active after being picked. It takes in oxygen, breaks down sugar and releases CO_2 at a much higher rate than other vegetables. When shopping, look for it to be stored in ice and cook it the day of purchase to capitalize on its health benefits.

JOHANNACASLER *Fitness*

The
Wild Side

SIDE DISHES

Gluten Free

Guiltless Pleasure

YIELDS: 6 servings | **SERVING SIZE:** 6 onion rings

INGREDIENTS:
1 large Red Onion
2 large Eggs
½ cup Almond Flour

PREPARATION:
Slice onion into thin rings. Beat 2 eggs in bowl. Dip onion slices in egg and dredge through almond flour. Lightly spray baking sheet with canola oil and bake at 425° for approximately 6 minutes, turn and cook an additional 4 minutes or until golden brown.

RECIPE RATING:

1   2   3   4   5

NUTRITION POINTS:
Aprox 120 calories + 24 gm protein per serving

Onions have many health benefits. They improve the working of vitamin C in the body. They contain chromium which assists in regulating blood sugar. They reduce inflammation and can assist in healing infections. Studies have shown they can help increase bone density. They are naturally low in calories **Almond Flour** is gluten free and gives a heart healthy protein boost **DON'T TOSS THE YOLKS! USE THE WHOLE EGG!** The egg yolk contains the bulk of the nutrients. Egg yolks are an excellent source of choline, which is the back bone of a nervous system neurotransmitter called acetylcholine. The part of the nervous system that runs your heart and keeps your intestines flowing relies heavily on acetylcholine.

JOHANNACASLER
Fitness

Guiltless
Pleasure

Gluten Free

Heavenly Eggs

YIELDS: 6 servings | **SERVING SIZE:** 2 egg halves

INGREDIENTS:
6 large Eggs
1 tsp Prepared Horseradish
¼ cup Plain Greek Yogurt
2 tsp Sweet Pickle Relish
½ tsp Garlic Salt
1 tsp Smoked Paprika

RECIPE RATING:
⭐ ⭐ ⭐ ⭐ ⭐
1 2 3 4 5

PREPARATION:
Place eggs in a pot of water with 3 inches over the eggs. Cook on high heat and bring to a rolling boil. Turn off heat, place lid on the pot and let sit for 15 minutes. Remove eggs with a slotted spoon into a bowl of cold water. Peel eggs under running water. Slice the eggs in half *(lengthwise)*, remove yolks and place in bowl, set aside egg white halves. Mash the yolks with a fork, add horseradish, garlic salt, relish and yogurt then mix well. Fill in the egg white halves with the mixture. Sprinkle with paprika.

NUTRITION POINTS:
Aprox 70 calories + 10 gm protein per serving

Egg Yolk contains the bulk of an egg's nutrients. They are an excellent source of choline which is the back bone of a nervous system neurotransmitter called acetylcholine. The part of the nervous system that runs your heart and keeps your intestines flowing relies heavily on acetylcholine. Vitamins A, D, E & K are found in the yolks. The natural fat in the yolks help the body absorb those fat soluble vitamins **Fermented Foods** such as Greek yogurt contribute to gut health and a good source of calcium and vitamin D **Paprika** is a super spice with anti-inflammatory benefits **Horseradish and Pickle Relish** add flavor with very little calories.

HEAVENLY eggs

Gluten Free

Mega Melons

SERVINGS: 1 serving

INGREDIENTS:
1 cup   Watermelon, cubed
1 oz   Sunflower Seeds

PREPARATION:
Take alternate bites and enjoy! The best snacks contain a quality carbohydrate, protein and a healthy fat for a nutrition trifecta. Fruit alone can cause a spike in blood sugar. Elevated blood sugar can signal the liver to produce cholesterol, cause inflammation and stimulate the production of visceral fat, the unhealthy fat surrounding your organs.

RECIPE RATING:

1   2   3   4   5

NUTRITION POINTS:
Aprox 200 calories + 6 gm protein per serving

Watermelon contains a host of vitamins and minerals. It has more lycopene than any other fruit or vegetable. It contains the amino acid L-citrulline which research shows improves recovery time and reduces muscle soreness from exercise **Sunflower Seeds** provide healthy fat, protein and a good source of potassium and vitamin E.

JOHANNACASLER
Fitness

MEGA
Melons
SNACK

Gluten Free

Mighty Mouth Poppers

YIELDS: 4 servings | **SERVING SIZE:** 2 poppers

INGREDIENTS:
4 ea   Jalapeños 🌶
12 tsp Goat Cheese *(1½ tsp per jalapeno half)*
8 tbsp Pancetta *(1 tbsp per jalapeno half)*

PREPARATION:
Slice jalapeños in half and core. Cook pancetta in pan until crisp. Remove from pan with a slotted spoon, then set pan with drippings aside. Fill jalapeños with goat cheese and top with pancetta. Place the jalapeños back in the pan drippings and apply medium heat for aprox 5 minutes.

RECIPE RATING:

1   2   3   4   5

NUTRITION POINTS:
Aprox 76 calories + 12 gm protein per serving

Jalapeños are a good source of vitamin A & C. They have an active compound called capsaicin, which gives the peppers their heat. Recent research suggests this compound can boost your metabolism **Goat cheese** is lower in calories than regular cheese and is a good source of vitamins A, K, calcium and protein. For some, it can be easier to digest than cow's milk **Pancetta**, also know as Italian bacon, is not smoked as most American bacon. Pancetta is typically cured in salt and spices and then dried for a few months. It has 9 gm of protein per 2 oz.

JOHANNACASLER
Fitness

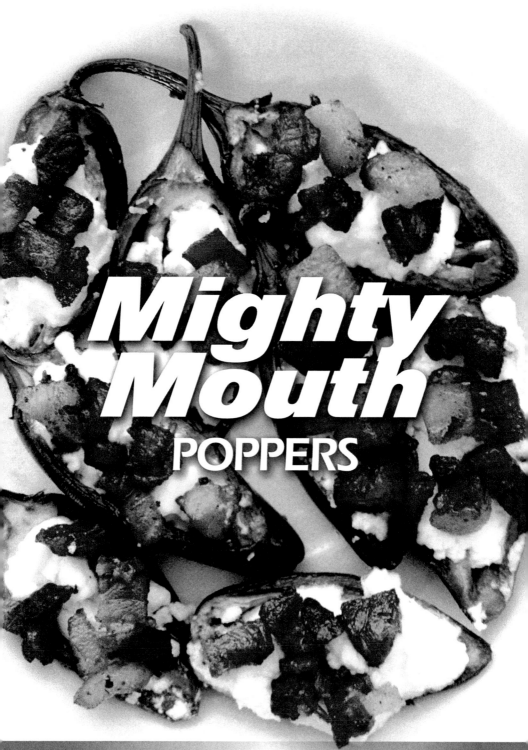

Mighty Mouth
POPPERS

S N A C K S

Energy Clusters

YIELDS: 8 servings | **SERVING SIZE:** 3 clusters

INGREDIENTS:
3 cups High Protein Granola
¼ cup Almond Flour
1 cup Peanut Butter, smooth or crunchy
1 tbsp Cinnamon, ground

PREPARATION:
Mix ingredients thoroughly in a bowl. Scoop spoon size portions onto wax paper. Freeze for 2 hours before serving. Store bites in freezer. *These are great with fruit, yogurt or as is!*

RECIPE RATING:

NUTRITION POINTS:
Aprox 120 calories + 12 gm protein per serving

These bites are a great snack for **Pre *or* Post-workouts** · **Almond Flour** gives a protein boost, is heart healthy and naturally gluten free · **Peanut Butter** adds protein, vitamins, great taste and helps bind the ingredients · **Granola** is a great source of quality carbohydrates · **Cinnamon** helps protect against blood sugar spikes.

ENERGY Clusters
SNACK

SNACKS

Fat Attack Snack

YIELDS: 1 serving

INGREDIENTS:
½ cup   Raspberries
½ cup   Blueberries
½ cup   Apples, chopped
1 ea   Kiwi, sliced
2 ea   **Energy Clusters** *(see previous recipe)*

PREPARATION:
Rinse and drain berries. Rinse and chop apple. Peel and slice kiwi.
Mix the fruit together and top with 2 crumbled **Energy Clusters**.

RECIPE RATING:

1   2   3   4   5

NUTRITION POINTS:
Aprox 230 calories + 8 gm protein per serving

Raspberries are part of fascinating research that is suggesting they can increase the metabolism in fat cells. The phytonutrients called rheosmin *(also called raspberry ketone)* is said to increase enzyme activity, oxygen consumption and heat production in certain types of fat cells **Blueberries** have one of the highest antioxidant capacities of all fruit, vegetables and spices. Research has shown they contribute to a healthy nervous system, as well as to brain health ·
Kiwi is an excellent source of vitamin C, K & folate · **Apples** are a good source of the water soluble fiber pectin. The phytonutrients in apples can help stabilize blood sugar · **Energy Clusters** add the protein source to make this an outstanding snack.

JOHANNACASLER
Fitness

Fat Attack

SNACK

S N A C K S

Gluten Free

Power Cube Smoothie

YIELDS: 1 serving

INGREDIENTS:

1 scoop	Whey or Pea Protein Powder
1 cup	Spinach
1 cup	Kale
1 cup	Swiss Chard
2 cups	Coconut Water
1 cup	Pomegranate Seeds
1 cup	Pink Grapefruit
1½ tbsp	Real Maple Syrup

RECIPE RATING:

1　　2　　3　　4　　5

PREPARATION:

STEP 1: **Power Cubes** – Prepare power cubes by blanching the 3 greens in boiling water for 1 minute. Drain, chop and fill ice cube trays with greens. Cover with water and freeze to make the Power Cubes. *Add them to soups, pasta dishes, etc. STEP 2:* **Smoothie** – Blend 5 prepared cubes and all remaining ingredients, then pour in a glass and enjoy.

NUTRITION POINTS:

Aprox 250 calories + 30 gm protein per serving

Power Cubes set this smoothie recipe apart from the rest. Greens have become a trendy part to smoothie and juicing recipes ▪ **Power Greens** have important nutrients, but to absorb those nutrients efficiently they need to be lightly cooked. Ingested raw, the bulk of the nutrients pass through the digestive system unabsorbed ▪ **Coconut Water** is low in calories, has more potassium than 4 bananas and has electrolytes that make it super hydrating ▪ **Grapefruit** is an excellent source of vitamin C and a good source of lycopene ▪ **Pomegranate Seeds** are full of vitamins, minerals, antioxidants and are anti-inflammatory ▪ **Real Maple Syrup** has 54 antioxidants and is a good source of zinc and manganese which are immune boosters.

POWER
CUBE
SMOOTHIE

INFUSED WATER

Refreshing Infused Water tastes great, can increase your daily water intake and add a nutrition boost. Get creative and make your own, just add ingredients to water and chill for at least 2 hours. *Enjoy!*

Strawberry Basil *(4 hrs to infuse)*

INGREDIENTS:

1 cup	Strawberries, sliced
¼ cup	Basil Leaves, halved
½ gal	Filtered Water

NUTRITION POINTS:

Berries are low calorie and offer antioxidant properties plus great flavor • **Basil** is a super herb contributing anti-bacterial, antioxidant and anti-inflammatory properties • **Shop** for organic berries and herbs.

Lemon Thyme Turmeric

INGREDIENTS:

1 large	Lemon, sliced
4 sprigs	Thyme
1 tbsp	Turmeric, grated
½ gal	Filtered Water

NUTRITION POINTS:

Lemon Juice helps cleanse the liver and has antioxidant and antibiotic properties • **Thyme** provides antioxidants, a great source of vitamins A & C and the minerals iron, copper and manganese • **Turmeric** is a powerful anti-inflammatory.

Lemon Ginger Mint

INGREDIENTS:

1 large	Lemon, sliced
4 sprigs	Mint
1 tbsp	Ginger, grated
½ gal	Filtered Water

NUTRITION POINTS:

Lemon Juice helps cleanse the liver and has antioxidant and antibiotic properties • **Ginger** aids digestion and boosts the immune system • **Mint** aids digestion and is a natural anti-inflammatory.

JOHANNACASLER
Fitness

Infused
Water

Made in the USA
San Bernardino, CA
21 September 2017